T0040954

ISBN 978-0-7935-9269-2

Disney characters and artwork © Disney Enterprises, Inc.

Wonderland Music Company, Inc. and Walt Disney Music Company

DISTRIBUTED BY

HAL•LEONARD®
CORPORATION
7777 W. BLUEMOUND RD. P.O. BOX 13819 MILWAUKEE, WI 53213

Visit Hal Leonard Online at
www.halleonard.com

CONTENTS

Can You Feel the Love Tonight

from Walt Disney Pictures' THE LION KING

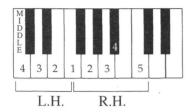

Music by Elton John
Lyrics by Tim Rice

Peacefully

Chorus: Can you feel the love to - night,

the peace the eve - ning brings? The world, for once, in per - fect har-mo-ny with

Duet Part (Student plays one octave higher than written.)
Peacefully

Go the Distance
from Walt Disney Pictures' HERCULES

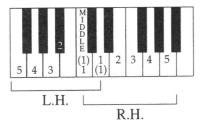

L.H.

R.H.

Music by Alan Menken
Lyrics by David Zippel

Moderate Ballad tempo

Young Hercules: I have of - ten dreamed of a

mp

far - off place where a great warm wel - come will be wait - ing for me. Where the

Duet Part (Student plays one octave higher than written.)

Moderate Ballad tempo

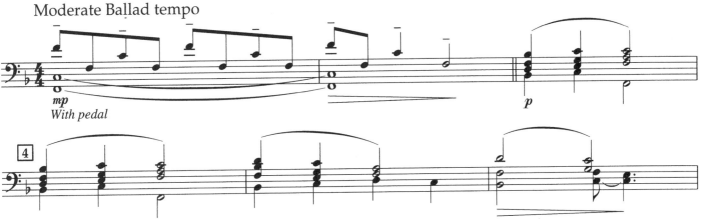

mp
With pedal

p

if I can be strong. I know ev - 'ry mile will be

worth my ____ while. I would go most an - y - where to

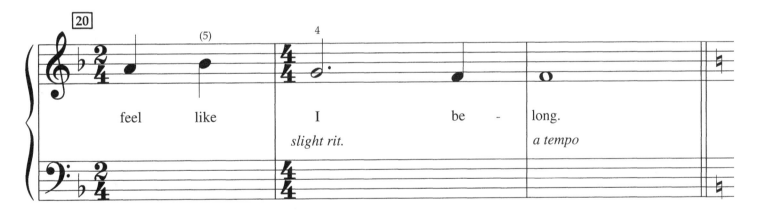

feel like I be - long.

slight rit. *a tempo*

slight rit. *a tempo*

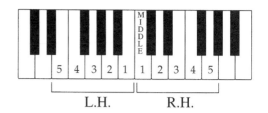

I am on my way.

mf

I can go the dis - tance, I don't care how far,

mp

10

Chim Chim Cher-ee
from Walt Disney's MARY POPPINS

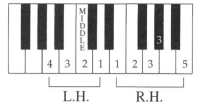

Words and Music by Richard M. Sherman
and Robert B. Sherman

Easily, with lilt

Chim chim-in-ey, chim chim-in-ey, chim chim cher-ee! A

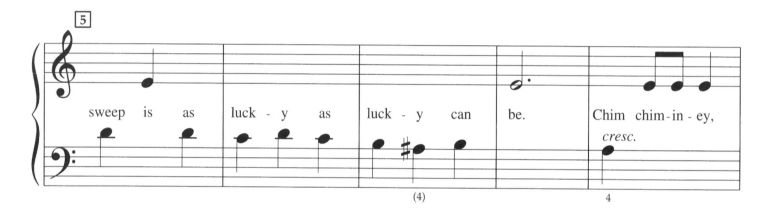

sweep is as luck-y as luck-y can be. Chim chim-in-ey,

Duet Part (Student plays one octave higher than written.)

Easily, with lilt

chim chim-in-ey, chim chim cher-oo! Good luck will rub

off when I shake hands with you. Or blow me a

mf

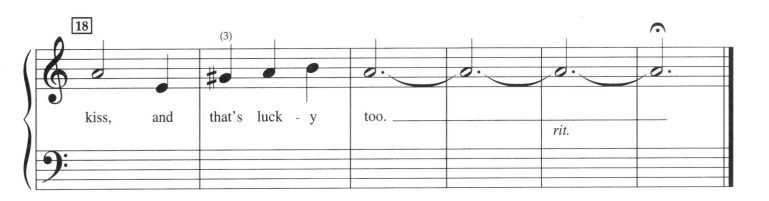

(3)

kiss, and that's luck-y too.

rit.

It's a Small World
from Disneyland and Walt Disney World's IT'S A SMALL WORLD

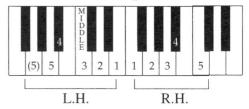

L.H.   R.H.

Words and Music by Richard M. Sherman
and Robert B. Sherman

Spirited

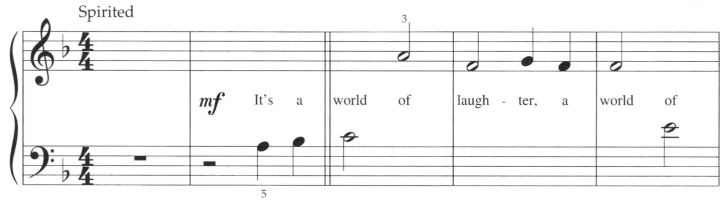

mf It's a world of laugh-ter, a world of

tears; it's a world of hopes and a world of fears. There's so

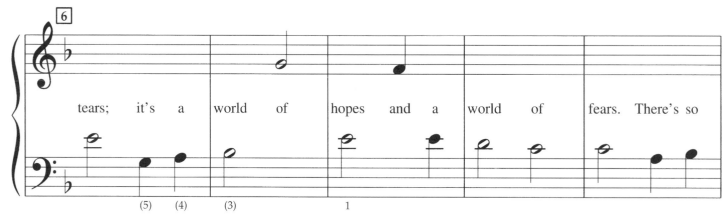

Duet Part (Student plays one octave higher than written.)

Spirited

much that we share that it's time we're a - ware it's a

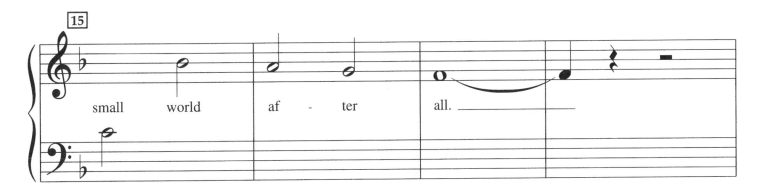

small world af - ter all.

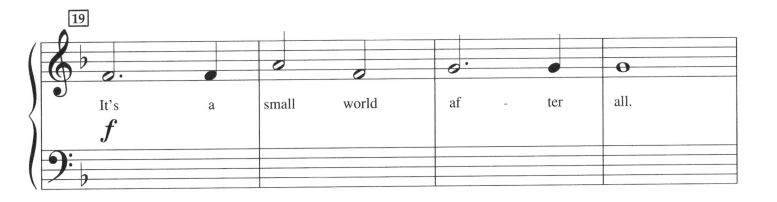

It's a small world af - ter all.

f

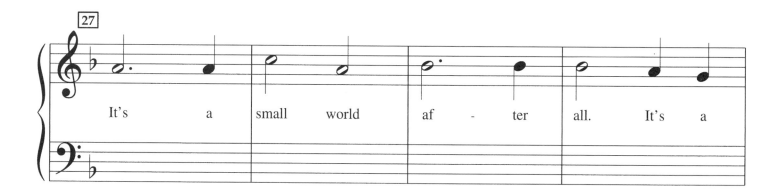

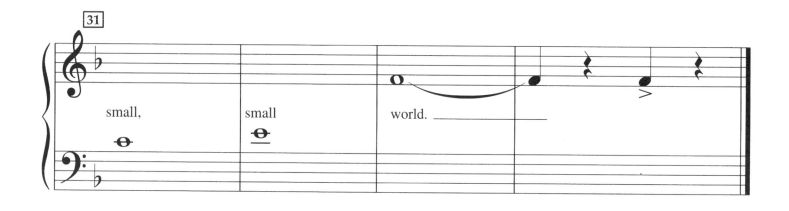

Supercalifragilisticexpialidocious

from Walt Disney's MARY POPPINS

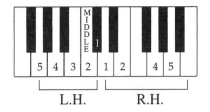

Words and Music by Richard M. Sherman
and Robert B. Sherman

Spirited

Su - per - cal - i - frag - il - is - tic -

Duet Part (Student plays one octave higher than written.)

Spirited

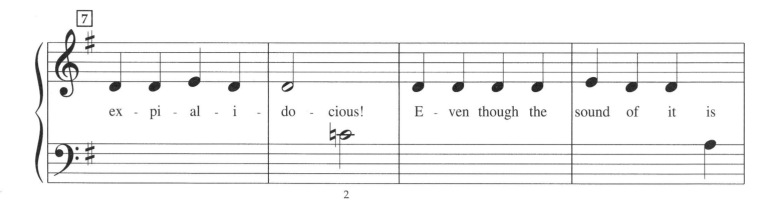

ex - pi - al - i - do - cious! E - ven though the sound of it is

2

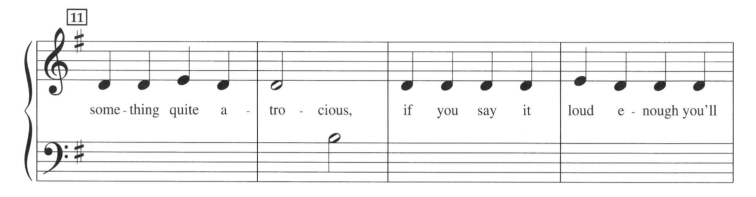

some - thing quite a - tro - cious, if you say it loud e - nough you'll

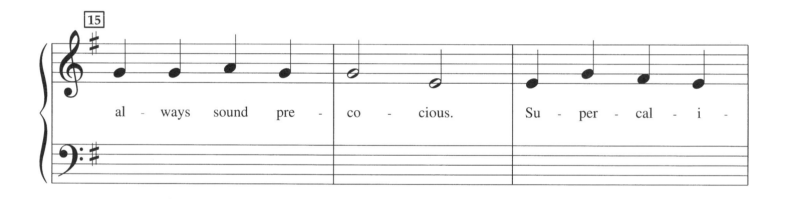

al - ways sound pre - co - cious. Su - per - cal - i -

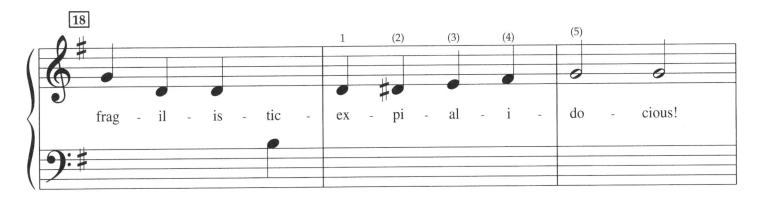

frag - il - is - tic - ex - pi - al - i - do - cious!

Under the Sea
from Walt Disney's THE LITTLE MERMAID

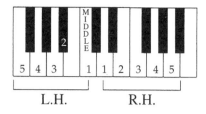

Lyrics by Howard Ashman
Music by Alan Menken

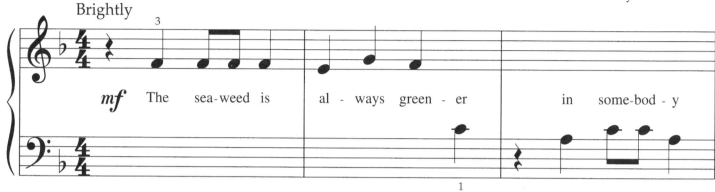

Duet Part (Student plays one octave higher than written.)

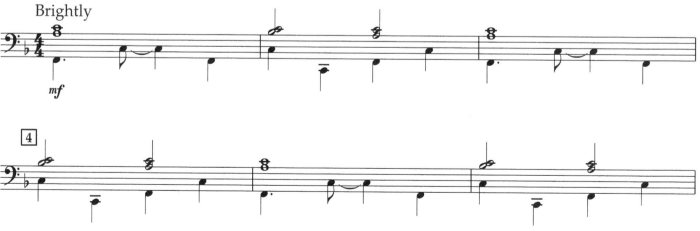

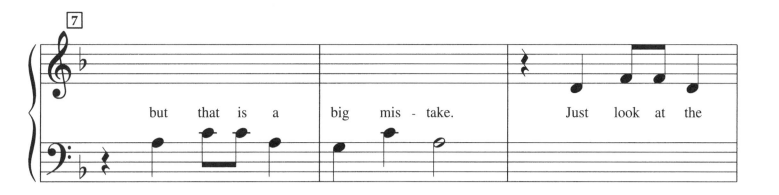

but that is a big mis-take. Just look at the

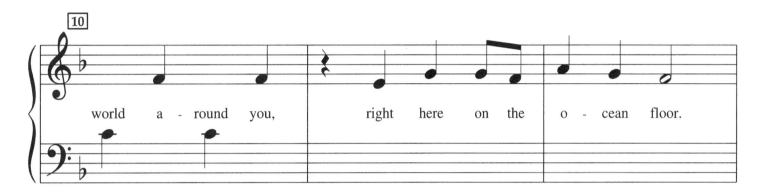

world a - round you, right here on the o - cean floor.

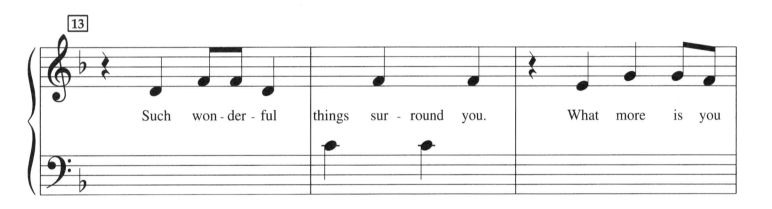

Such won-der-ful things sur-round you. What more is you

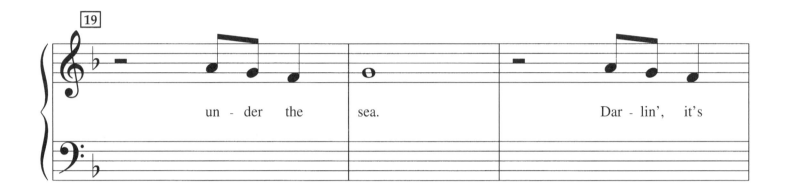

Up on the shore they work all day. Out in the

sun they slave a - way. While we de - vot - in' full time to

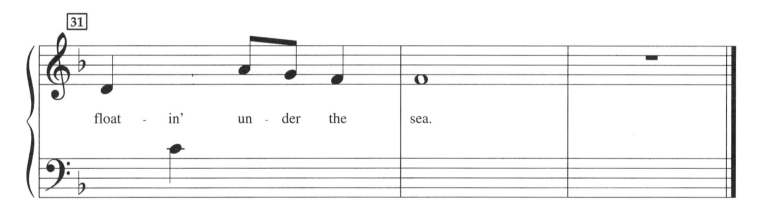

float - in' un - der the sea.

You've Got a Friend in Me

from Walt Disney's TOY STORY

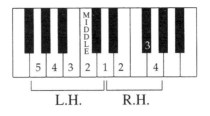

Music and Lyrics by
Randy Newman

With a swing

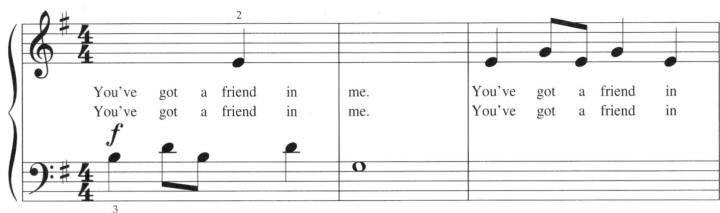

You've got a friend in me.
You've got a friend in me.
You've got a friend in
You've got a friend in

me.
me.
When the road looks rough a - head and you're
You got troubles, then I got 'em ___ too.

Duet Part (Student plays one octave higher than written.)

With a swing

miles _ and miles from your nice warm bed,
There isn't any - thing I wouldn't do for you.

you just re - mem-ber what your
If we stick to - geth - er we can

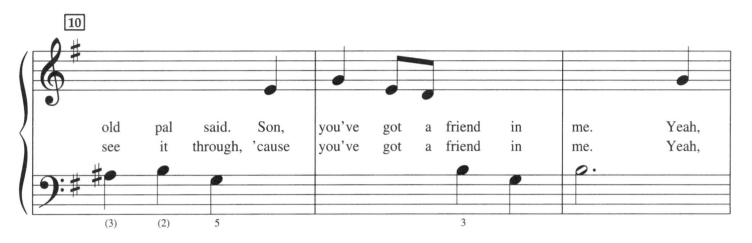

old pal said. Son, you've got a friend in me. Yeah,
see it through, 'cause you've got a friend in me. Yeah,

(3) (2) 5 3

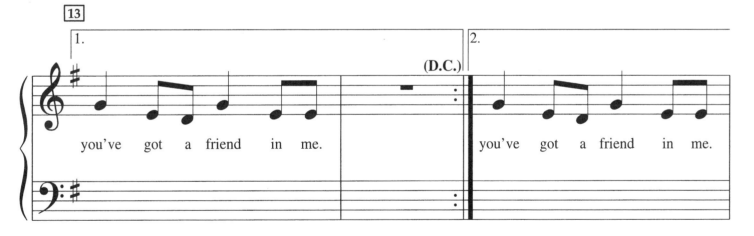

1. (D.C.) 2.

you've got a friend in me. you've got a friend in me.

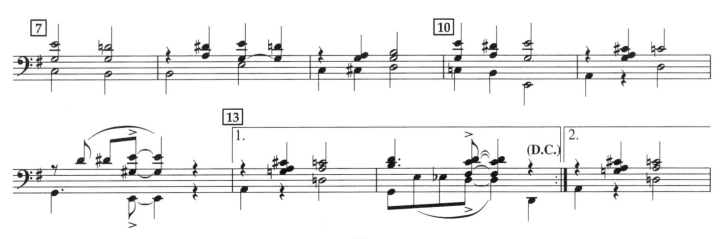

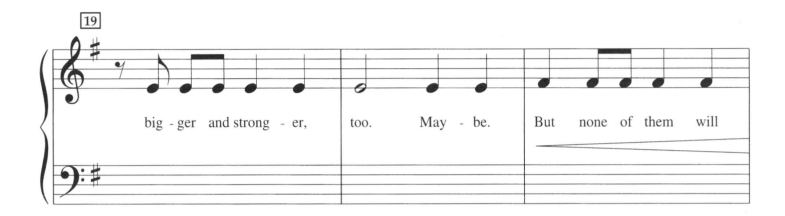

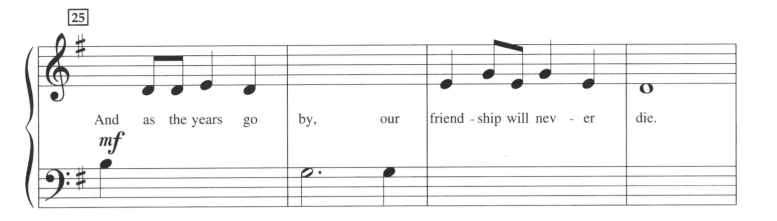

And as the years go by, our friend - ship will nev - er die.

mf

You're gon-na see it's our des - ti - ny. You've got a friend in me.

molto rit. *f* *a tempo*

You've got a friend in me. You've got a friend in me.

mf *f*

mp

molto rit.

mf
a tempo

mp

mf

Zero to Hero
from Walt Disney Pictures' HERCULES

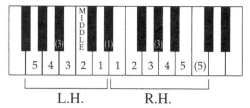

L.H.   R.H.

Music by Alan Menken
Lyrics by David Zippel

Brightly

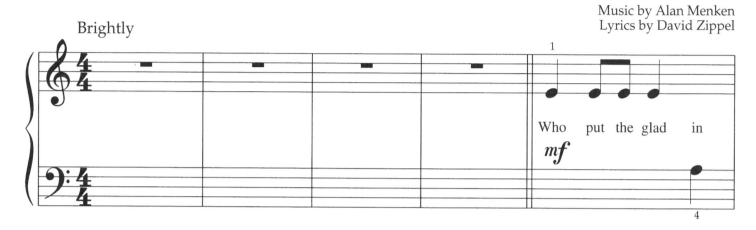

Who put the glad in

mf

glad - i - a - tor?   Her - cu - les.   Whose

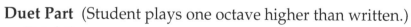

Duet Part (Student plays one octave higher than written.)

Brightly

mf

mp

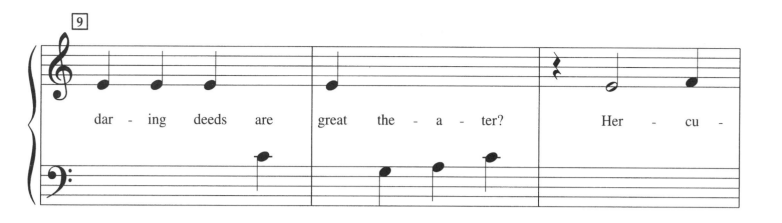

dar - ing deeds are great the - a - ter? Her - cu -

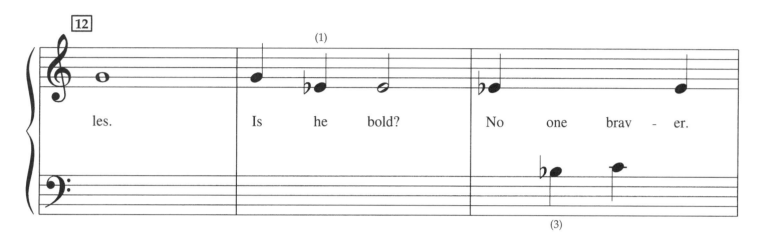

les. Is he bold? No one brav - er.

Is he sweet? Our fav - 'rite fla - vor. Her - cu -

f

mf

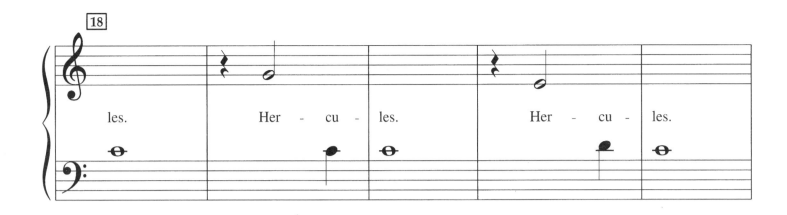

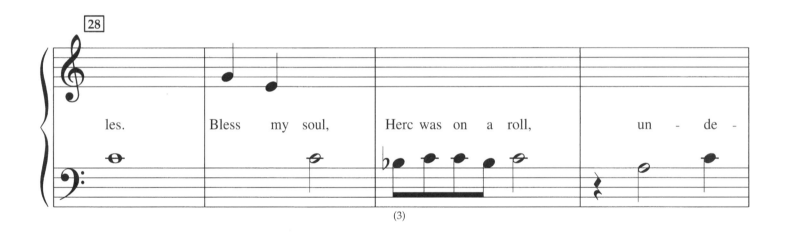

(3)

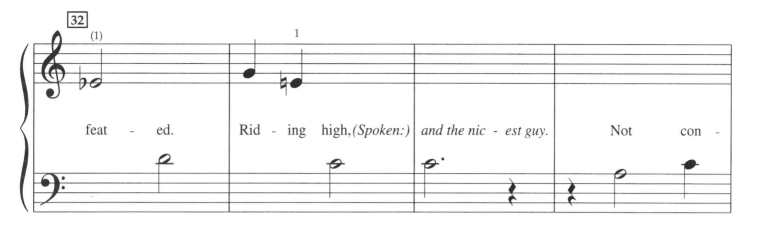

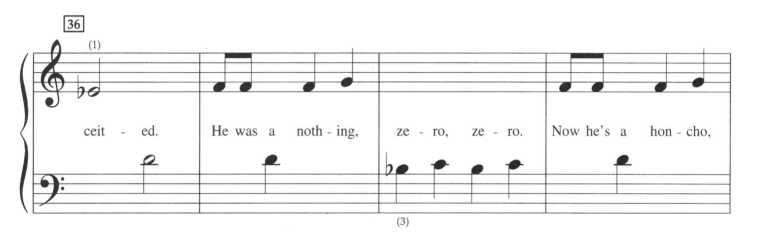

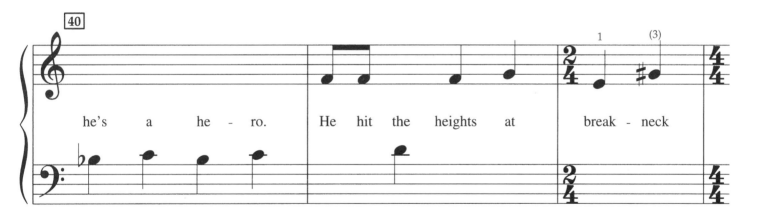

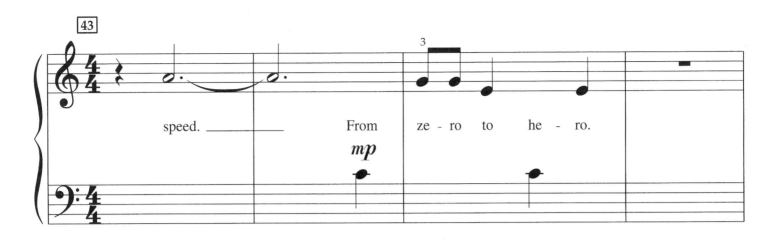

speed. _____ From ze - ro to he - ro.

mp

Herc is a he - ro. Now he's a he - ro. ____

mf *f*

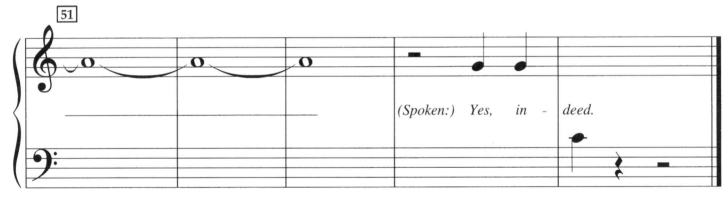

(Spoken:) Yes, in - deed.